DATE DUE			

Contents

Chapter 1

Dreams and Confessions

On the night of June 1, 2003, Stephenie Meyer had a dream that changed her life forever.[1] Her nocturnal visions were of an average teenage girl and a gorgeous, sparkling vampire with butterscotch eyes. They were alone in a meadow. They spoke of their yearning and affection for each other. The vampire promised not to hurt her. She declared her feelings for him by saying, "I would rather die than stay away from you."[2]

The dream was so vivid and captivating that after Meyer woke, she stayed in bed longer than usual just to think about what she had seen. It was such a fantastic dream that she did not want to forget it.

After washing and dressing, Meyer went to her computer and typed out the dream. She did not have names for the love struck teen couple and simply used the generic "he" and "she" while writing out descriptions of her visions.[3] She forged ahead and wrote as much as she could remember about the nameless lovers. "The core of the dream that I had was this sense of this innocent and unselfish love that is going on, but with the undercurrent of his natural desire to kill her."[4] Meyer was so inspired by the scene and the characters that she wrote ten more pages.[5]

After fleshing out the initial meadow scene, Meyer wrote every day for three months. "Once I'd written everything that I'd dreamed, I was eager to know more about what would happen to these intriguing characters. So I kept typing, letting the story go where it wanted to go."[6]

> ## "Once I'd written everything that I'd dreamed, I was eager to know more . . ."

When it came to naming her romantic duo, Meyer had an easier time finding the perfect name for her vampire character than she did for her love-bitten girl character. "I decided to use a name that had once been considered romantic, but had fallen out of popularity for decades."[7] The name Edward had been used in two classic romance novels. In Charlotte Bronte's *Jane Eyre* (1847), Edward Rochester was the novel's central male character. In Jane Austen's novel *Sense and Sensibility* (1811), Edward Ferrars was the wealthy leading man.

Meyer tried the name for her teen vampire and found it was a perfect fit for the perfect vampire. Edward Cullen, eternal heartthrob of young adult literature, was born. But when it came to finding a name for her lead girl, Meyer stated, "Nothing I named her seemed just right. After spending so much time with her, I loved her like a daughter, and no name was good enough. Finally, inspired by that love, I gave her the name I was saving for my daughter." Isabella.[8]

Meyer's main character, Isabella Swan, is often referred to as Bella, which means "beauty" or "sweetheart" in Italian. Edward is drawn to Bella's loveliness, innocence, and her irresistible scent. Bella is enchanted by everything about Edward: his dazzling smile, statuesque build, and his ever-lasting life.

Meyer's vivid dream became a story and that story became her obsession. "Not a day passed that I didn't write something—I couldn't keep myself away from the computer," she wrote on her publisher's Web site. "On bad days, I would type out a page or two; on good days, I would finish a chapter and then some."[9]

While Meyer expanded her dream into the full-length story of Bella and Edward, she was simply writing for her own entertainment. She was twenty-nine and the mother of three boys under five years

This scene from the 2008 film adaptation of *Twilight* captures the imagery of Stephenie Meyer's original dream which inspired the entire story.

old. Being an author had never even crossed her mind.

In a 2006 interview, Meyer stated, "I wrote *Twilight* over the summer of 2003. I didn't think about publishing at all until it was entirely done— I was just telling myself a story. Writing just for the sake of writing, just for my own pleasure."[10] But as it turned out, those first ten pages that were written on June 2, 2003, later became "Confessions"—chapter 13 of her blockbuster first novel, *Twilight*.

It took Meyer only three short months to write *Twilight*. That is an amazing accomplishment for any writer. Writing a 498-page novel is a huge commitment and undertaking for anyone. Add three rambunctious boys and it becomes clear how driven Stephenie Meyer had to be in order to finish the book. Meyer recalled her writing process and stated it was "an unusual experience because I felt so obsessive about the process. It wasn't like me to be so focused—it's hard to be with all the kids around."[11]

To balance her writing and family time, she spent a lot of time working on the story at night while her children were asleep. Her sons were five, two, and one years old. Writing after their bedtime made it easier for her to concentrate and allowed her to have hours of uninterrupted time.

On September 17, 2008, Meyer appeared on the *Ellen DeGeneres Show* and spoke of her nighttime schedule. "I didn't have a lot of time. I lost a lot of sleep." Even though writing in the dark of night seems fitting for an author of a vampire romance, there were also times when Meyer wrote during the day. She found it difficult to stay away from her computer. She juggled writing and motherhood by writing a few sentences between cups of juice and diaper changes.[12] "I did a lot of writing with my one-year-old on my lap. He's kind of a monkey so he could cling and I would type around him."

Sometime in June 2003, shortly after Meyer began writing *Twilight*, she started sending chapters to her older sister, Emily. Emily encouraged Meyer by checking in with her and asking for more chapters to read.[13] It is fair to say that her older sister became her very first fan. Meyer continued to send pages to Emily but had no intention of publishing the story. "I wasn't planning on publishing it. It was for an audience of one," Meyer said.[14]

Meyer's mindset changed after the novel was completed in August 2003, and Emily suggested she should try to get it published. With the hefty manuscript finished, and the thumbs up from her big sister, Meyer began to research how to get a book published. Less than four months passed when Meyer was offered her first staggering book deal with publisher Little, Brown and Company. In September 2005, *Twilight* would go from an audience of one to a first printing of seventy-five thousand hardcover copies.

Little, Brown and Company's 2005 catalog described *Twilight* as follows:

> Isabella Swan's move to Forks, a small, perpetually rainy town in Washington, could have been the most boring move she ever made. But once she meets the mysterious and alluring Edward Cullen, Isabella's life takes a thrilling and terrifying turn. Up until now, Edward has managed to keep his vampire identity a secret in the small community he lives in, but now nobody is safe, especially Isabella, the person Edward holds most dear.
>
> The lovers find themselves balanced precariously on the point of a knife—between desire and danger. Deeply romantic and extraordinarily suspenseful, *Twilight* captures the struggle between defying our instincts and satisfying our desires. This is a love story with bite.

Stephenie Meyer described the storyline by saying, "[I]t's mostly about a vampire who falls in love with a normal human girl. And sort of the inherent problems with dating vampires."[15]

Like many classic and modern love stories, the characters in *Twilight* struggle with falling for someone who is considered an outsider. In William Shakespeare's *Romeo and Juliet*, the Capulets and the Montagues are two feuding families. After a romantic flirtation, Juliet Capulet learns that Romeo is a Montague. She wails to her nurse, "My only love sprung from my only hate."

Authors have used the "opposites attract" theme in books for decades. In Meyer's love story, Edward and Bella have more obstacles to overcome compared to other romantic literary couples.

In *Twilight*'s meadow scene, Edward Cullen states their romantic dilemma perfectly to Bella. "And so the lion fell in love with the lamb." Bella looks away in an attempt to hide how thrilled she is that he used the word *love*. A few sentences later, sunlight glints off of his teeth.

Meyer definitely turned the tension up a notch when she paired a beautiful, ageless vampire with a typical high-school girl. Falling madly in love and grappling with their differences makes for a thrilling, blood-pumping page-turner.

Chapter 2

"Here's the Story . . ."

It was December 24, 1973, when Candy and Stephen Morgan welcomed their second child into the world. On that Christmas Eve, they named their baby girl Stephenie, as a way to honor her father. From then on, she would forever be known as "Stephenie," instead of the more common spelling of "Stephanie."

At the time Stephenie was born, the Morgans and their oldest daughter, Emily, were living in Hartford, Connecticut. Hartford is recognized as one of America's original cities. It was founded in the early 1600s by Dutch traders. Today, the city's slogan pronounces Hartford as "New England's Rising Star."

Located in the northeast region of the United States, Connecticut is a state with distinct seasons.

In winter, the average temperature in January is a chilly 25 degrees Fahrenheit. Stephenie only had to endure the cold and bundle up for a few winters. When she was four years old, the family relocated to the warmer climate in Phoenix, Arizona, where the average coldest temperature in January is 45 degrees. The hottest month is usually July when average temperatures can hit 107 degrees.

Once the family settled in Phoenix, Stephen Morgan provided for his family by working as a finance manager.[1] As the family continued to grow, Stephenie and Emily welcomed four younger siblings into the household, bringing the Morgan children to a total of six: Emily, Stephenie, Heidi, Jacob, Paul, and Seth.

The Morgan family was very close-knit and they spent a lot of time together. Looking back on her childhood, Stephenie once said, "When you grow up in a big family, there's always someone to hang out with."[2] Being the second oldest, Stephenie helped out with younger kids by babysitting and changing diapers.[3]

Growing up with two sisters and three brothers, Stephenie has compared the Morgan children to the six characters on the 1970s television sitcom *The Brady Bunch*. Considering she was also the second oldest of the three girls, Stephenie said, "I filled the Jan Brady spot in my family."[4]

Like *The Brady Bunch*, the Morgans also had a family dog. That is where the similarities between the fictional television family and the Morgans ended. Stephenie's dog was named Eagle and the Brady dog was called Tiger.

Joking about the comparison between her mother and the ultra-perfect Mrs. Brady, Stephenie said, "We never had a maid, so my mom is clearly superior to Florence Henderson's character, and also has a better singing voice."[5]

In a 2006 interview, Stephenie spoke about how growing up with two sisters and three brothers influenced her writing. She stated, "I think that coming from such a large family has given me a lot of insight into different personality types—my siblings sometimes crop up as characters in my stories."[6]

Outside of her family, Stephenie was also influenced a great deal by her faith. As a member of the Church of Jesus Christ of Latter-day Saints, also known as Mormons, Stephenie credits her religious beliefs for helping her become who she is and form her perspective on the world.[7]

Stephenie studied the Book of Mormon, which is described by the church as "a second witness of Jesus Christ and a companion volume of scripture to the Bible that records God's dealings with the ancient inhabitants of the Americas." She also read the New Testament several times and read the entire Old Testament once.[8]

Stephenie attended Chaparral High School in Scottsdale, Arizona. Some might imagine that she spent her teen years lurking in graveyards or hanging out with a Goth crowd, but in reality, her high-school years were pretty typical.

Her friends consisted of girls who came from various religious backgrounds. Looking back on her teen years, she said, "[It] was me, the crazy Mormon, . . . the hippie-raised Atheist, . . . the Jewish girl . . . , the Baptist . . . , and then . . . the quiet Lutheran. We had some pretty mind-boggling religious discussions."[9]

As a self-proclaimed late bloomer, Stephenie admitted, "When I was sixteen, holding hands was just—wow."[10] She was more interested in cars than boys and recalled, "My friends used to follow cute boys on the highway, while I would follow cars."[11] When asked about her "good girl" reputation, Stephenie stated it was expected in the community she grew up in. "And all of my friends were good girls too, and my boyfriends were good boys."[12]

Stephenie attended the Chaparral High School prom with KJ, a boy she became friends with during morning church classes. The night of the dance, Stephenie wore a purple knee-length dress. Her date dressed in a tuxedo and wore a bow tie that matched her dress. A dinner was held at KJ's house where the couple was served lemon chicken. KJ did not have money to rent a limo, so he drove Stephenie to the dance in his Dad's Mercury Sable. Before they left, they posed for a few photographs.[13] Arm in arm, the pair smiled for the camera. Her wrist corsage matched his boutonniere. He was several inches taller than she. They appeared to be a couple of happy teenagers who were excited about their high-school prom.

Because they were teens and low on cash, the few snapshots taken at KJ's house are all that exist

Kemery Judd and Stephenie Morgan prior to the Chaparral High School prom in 1992.

of their prom night. KJ did not have funds to pay the photographer for professional shots at the dance.[14] Even though Stephenie did not know it at the time, it would be many years before she would have another opportunity to attend a prom and be the belle of the ball.

In a brief online interview in 2007, author and friend Shannon Hale asked Stephenie to describe her teen self: "Geeky, quiet (as in: 'She was a quiet girl, kept to herself . . .'), and book-obsessed."[15]

It would seem likely that Stephenie would have read hoards of vampire novels as a teenager, but that is not the case. In fact, she has described herself as a "total chicken. . . . I've never read a Stephen King book in my life. . . . I really don't like gore; I hate the slasher type of thing."[16]

As a teenager, Stephenie's favorite books were *Pride and Prejudice* and *Gone With the Wind*. "I was reading big books from the time when I was little."[17] She was just nine years old when she read *Jane Eyre* by Charlotte Bronte. Stephenie reread the book so many times that she developed a kinship toward the main character. "Jane was someone I was close to as a child—we were good friends! I think in some ways she was more real to me than any other fictional heroine."[18]

Just as Stephenie had a dislike for scary books, she also never cared for creepy movies either. One movie she did watch a lot as a kid was *Somewhere in Time*. It featured the handsome actor Christopher Reeve and the beautiful Jane Seymour. Released in 1980, the movie was a romantic drama with a fantasy element. The music in the movie made an impression on Stephenie as well. "Every time you hear that song, you're poised to fall in love. The relationship there is just this impossible thing that he makes possible." Recognizing that the movie helped inspire her writing life, Stephenie remarked, "That had to be an influence on me."[19]

Growing up, Stephenie's family, friends, upbringing, school, church, and even the books and movies she entertained herself with, all played a part in forming who she would become as an adult. In her adulthood, she would end up creating a main character that millions of teens would relate to and one who shares some of her own traits.

Comparing her teen self to *Twilight*'s heroine, Bella (Isabella) Swan, Stephenie said, "I think she has a few things in common with my own teenage self—the same sarcastic internal voice, the same shyness and wobbly self-confidence, and a few physical similarities, . . . I wish I would have known someone like her when I was seventeen. She would have been a good person to be friends with."[20]

Just as Stephenie became good friends with her favorite fictional heroine as a teen, the character she created in Bella Swan has done the same for countless readers around the world.

Chapter 3

Literature
and Love

After four years at Chaparral High School, Stephenie Morgan continued her education by enrolling in college. She had been awarded a National Merit Scholarship and used those funds to help pay for her tuition at Brigham Young University in Provo, Utah.

Receiving such an award is an honor. Scholarships are given to select students as a way to recognize their hard work. As described on their Web site:

> The National Merit Scholarship Program is an academic competition for recognition and scholarships that began in 1955. High school students enter the National Merit Program by taking the Preliminary SAT/National Merit Scholarship Qualifying Test—a test which serves as an initial screen of approximately 1.5 million entrants each year. . . .

In 1993, when Stephenie was twenty years old, she began dating Christian Meyer. Christian's nickname was Pancho, and he and Stephenie had known each other since they were four. Even though they attended church activities and social events as kids, they did not actually become friendly until they were out of their teens.[1] Some time passed before they saw one another again. "We'd both changed a little bit," Stephenie recalled. "He looks good!" was her reaction when she saw Pancho.[2]

Once they reconnected, their relationship became serious pretty quickly. Pancho proposed marriage on their second date and continued to propose. Stephenie described Pancho as the most self-confident person she had ever met.[3] "He proposed a lot. Over forty times." That was a boost to her insecurity, and she found herself drawn to his absolute surety. "He would propose every night and I would tell him no every night,"[4] Stephenie said. She finally said yes, and the two were married just nine months after their first date.

About two years after they married, the couple welcomed their first son, Gabe, into the world. It was a busy time for the young family. Stephenie earned her degree in English Literature and graduated from Brigham Young University with the class of 1997.

During her studies there, she focused more on literature and reading than on creative writing. By concentrating on literature, she was able to earn course credits by reading—something she would have been doing anyway.[5] Explaining why she chose to get an English degree, Meyer said, "That's what I love. I love reading, and this was a major I could read in."[6]

By age twenty-three, Meyer was settled in married life and raising Gabe. Pancho worked as an auditor in an accounting firm.[7] Meyer was a stay-at-home mom who also spent time with her scrapbook club. She continued with church activities and also enjoyed going to movies. She had done some painting in college but gave it up once she started a family.[8]

By the time her other two boys, Seth and Eli, were born, Meyer had read stacks and stacks of books. "I just read all the time. In fact, my husband used to tease me. I went through six years of always having a little baby in my arms, and so my other hand was pretty much shaped in the form of a book to hold it open. I probably read five to six novels a week."[9]

Meyer's taste in literature ranges from the classics to science fiction. She has said that the many authors who have influenced her include: William Shakespeare, L. M. Montgomery, Louisa May Alcott, Janet Evanovich, and Orson Scott Card. While many of those authors are well known and very popular, none of them have written vampire sagas.

By reading so much and spending her college years earning an English degree, Meyer probably did not realize it at the time, but she was gearing up to become a very popular author herself.

Chapter 4

Supermom

In 2002, Meyer was twenty-eight years old and spending much of her time taking care of her three young children. She seemed to be living a typical, normal life as a mom and wife. She drove a mini-van and sewed fancy Halloween costumes for her boys.[1]

Motherhood brought Meyer a lot of happiness. As in most households, Meyer's days were most likely filled with chores, laundry, cooking, snack times, and nap times. As the boys grew older, they had fun playing video games and going to amusement parks.[2]

Meyer spoke about how being a mom deepened her compassion. "Everybody's somebody's kid, right?" she said. "So as a mom, compassion comes with the territory. You want people to be happy;

you want to understand them; you want them to be well-adjusted."[3]

Meyer's motherly instincts and compassion can be traced back to her childhood years. When she helped take care of her brothers by babysitting, she must have taken her duties very seriously. She has said that she had "Mom" nightmares about her brothers. When she became a mom herself, the dreams returned. "When you're a mom, you have nightmares about terrible things happening to your kids and you can't stop them."[4]

While most people have dreams about their loved ones, it is fair to assume that Meyer's dreams must have been extremely realistic and vivid. It could also be said that being a voracious reader influenced her nocturnal creativity. But even during the daytime, Meyer's mind created stories. "I was always a storyteller, though I only told my stories to myself," Meyer said in a 2006 interview.[5]

> **"I was always a storyteller, though I only told my stories to myself."**

As a well-educated, creative woman, Meyer probably did not think her imagination was out of the ordinary. Especially since, at this point, she had not had a dream that really struck her as something different and special.

Meyer reads from *Eclipse* in Cologne, Germany. As a young wife and mother, the possibility of achieving international fame never crossed Meyer's mind.

Meyer has said she is too chicken to read horror novels. She also does not watch R-rated movies.[6] That may be a result of her upbringing, but it is more likely due to her individual taste in movies and entertainment. She has always been a fan of superheroes. "This is crazy, but those Saturday morning cartoons . . . I was always fascinated with the X-Men." She admitted that the connection she felt with a group of animated superheroes had something to do with coming from a large family. "I always clicked into that kind of story."[7]

Meyer's family and her Mormon faith probably played a part in instilling conservative values in her. As a Mormon, Meyer does not drink alcohol. Explaining why that is important, she told a *Time* magazine reporter, "It's about keeping yourself free of addictions."[8] That includes addiction to caffeine—something else Mormons generally stay away from. Meyer does allow herself a Diet Pepsi once in a while, though.

Being a member of the Church of Jesus Christ of Latter-day Saints requires time and commitment. Besides attending three hours of church on Sundays, Meyer also taught Sunday school to a group of teenagers.[9] Talking about what the Mormon faith teaches, Meyer said, "We have free will, which is a huge gift from God." Some Mormons refer to free will as Free Agency or, simply, Agency, which is defined as "the ability and freedom to choose good or evil."[10]

Because of both of their upbringings, Meyer and her husband have a strong bond. She credits Pancho's mother for raising him to treat women as equals. "He expects the women in his life to have interests and opinions and a mind of her own. He can handle the fact that I am at least as strong a person as he is, and that I am smart and capable and often right."[11]

It seems the Meyer boys have a few things in

common with their mom. Once, while their mom was being interviewed by a reporter, they burst into the room. In typical boy fashion, Seth was wearing a superhero costume. He jumped onto the couch and explained he was "Animal Time," a hero he invented who has all the powers of the world's animals, and that he was able to talk to them, too. Meyer's youngest son, Eli, had a car book and proudly told them, "I know every car in the world." He also said his favorite car is the Porsche.[12]

Meyer has joked that her fun-loving boys "often remind me of chimpanzees on crack."[13] Looking back to when she began her writing career, she said, "I don't have any idea how I survived trying to do so many things at once."

Being a wife, mother of three, a regular church attendee, a Sunday-school teacher, and an aspiring author is a lot for one person. Watching Saturday morning cartoons certainly paid off for Meyer. It seems she learned a thing or two about being a superhero.

Chapter 5

Muse and Inspirations

Up until the morning that Meyer woke up with her vivid dream still running in her head, she had no desire to write a novel. Even on that June day in 2003, she simply wanted to write down the dream because she did not want to forget it. There were no plans to turn it into a book. She had no plans to change her career as a stay-at-home mom.

There was breakfast to be served and swimsuits to pack for the first day of swimming lessons for her young sons, but Meyer felt compelled to write the scene.[1] When she sat down at her computer that day, it had been years since she had written anything. She had done some writing in college, but this was the first time since her oldest son was born that she was writing for the simple pleasure of getting to know her characters.

Once the meadow scene dream and the first ten pages were down, Meyer could not stop writing. In 2007, Meyer spoke to a reporter for the Brigham Young University magazine and said, "I started out just so I wouldn't forget the story, but I kept going. I really felt like it was a situation where I had a talent I was not using; I had buried it. And that was my kick-start. I was supposed to be doing something with this talent."[2]

Meyer continued to go back to the story and add pages to it. She kept what she was doing a secret until her sister Emily got it out of her. It was unusual for Meyer to ignore e-mails and not return phone calls. Finally, Emily got ahold of her and asked Meyer, "What's going on? Why aren't you calling me anymore?"[3]

Meyer could not keep the secret from her big sister and ended up confiding in her. "I thought she'd laugh, but it turns out she's a big Buffy fan." The fact that Emily watched *Buffy the Vampire Slayer* put Meyer at ease. When Emily asked to read her novel in progress, Meyer took her up on it. "She wanted to see it, and, on the one hand, I was very shy about it, but on the other hand, I was in love with it, so I wanted her to see it."[4]

Meyer sent Emily chapters as the novel

> **"I was supposed to be doing something with this talent."**

progressed, and Emily was so into the story that she could hardly wait until the next chapter. She resorted to calling Meyer to bug and hound her to keep writing and send her more.

In order to make writing time, Meyer dropped out of her scrapbooking club. She was already a busy woman with a very full life and schedule, and free time was tight. "I became somewhat of a hermit that summer, neglecting friends, family, and my normal hobbies," she said, looking back.[5]

Writing is a solitary endeavor that takes commitment and time. Anyone who takes on a novel while raising a family also has to have a lot of energy. Meyer stole minutes to write a little during the day, but mostly she wrote after dark. She lost a lot of sleep in order to stay up to write after her kids were in bed. She was a woman on a mission and said the story poured out of her. "It gushed. On a good day I would write ten to twelve pages, single-spaced. That's a good chapter and then some. So it was coming very fast. And then there were other parts that were slower, but it pretty much flowed."[6]

In comparison to the scrapbooking hobby or painting she did years earlier, it was writing that clicked with Meyer's creative side. "When I switched to writing, it was a much fuller outlet for me. There was a whole lot of pleasure in that first writing experience. It felt like a dam bursting."[7]

When Meyer first began her story with the dream of the teenagers in the meadow, she followed that scene and wrote to the end. But by the time she wrote "The End," she understood her characters better and decided to begin their story differently. What had originally been chapter 1— "Confessions"—ended up being chapter 13 once she added twelve more chapters to the front of the book.[8]

By the time the end of August rolled around, Meyer typed her book's final sentence. Less than three months had passed between the start and finish of her first novel, *Twilight*. Managing to write what turned into a 498-page novel in that amount of time is astounding. Even with loss of sleep and contending with her reduced time, Meyer said it was one of the most enjoyable experiences of her life.[9] "It was really the writing process that made me a writer. I just had so much fun. It was better than the dream . . . getting to make it real."[10]

Meyer's main character, dark-haired seventeen-year-old Bella Swan, came to her fully formed in her dream. Being a living teenage girl who falls for a vampire is a story premise that provides lots of conflict for Bella. The conflicts and obstacles that Bella has to overcome to get what she wants make for the perfect ingredients when creating a character that readers will connect with.

Edward Cullen, the vampire who has been seventeen years old since 1918, has his own conflicts to contend with. He is drawn to Bella and fights the urge to do what vampires do—drink blood. In Edward, Meyer created a character that is tormented by his own desires and the safety of the one he loves.

Meyer did not write *Twilight* as anything but a romance—a romance that stars gorgeous heart-throbs who just happen to be vampires and werewolves. Meyer took a vulnerable girl and a gentleman vampire, and then she threw a sympathetic werewolf boy named Jacob Black into the mix to create a love triangle like no other.

Talking about her main men, Meyer said, "Edward is too perfect to exist in reality. I've known pieces of Jacob in various forms—he's much more likely to occur in nature. Much more human and much more possible."[11]

Choice is a recurring theme throughout *Twilight* and something both Bella and Edward struggle with. Edward and the rest of the Cullen family made the choice not to kill humans and instead hunt animals to quench their thirst for blood.

"Edward is too perfect to exist in reality."

Bella is constantly presented with choices to make. Some are more difficult than others: good or evil, love or friendship, life or death, humanity or immortality. After finishing the book, Meyer said, "Hopefully, most girls who read it will find something in Bella they can relate to."[12]

Even though Meyer did not intentionally weave Mormon beliefs within the story, she recognized there are subtle similarities. "Mormon themes do come through in *Twilight*. Free agency—I see that in the Cullens. The vampires made this choice to be something more—that's my belief, the importance of free will to be human."[13]

Meyer has admitted she can be kind of obsessive about her characters. It seems she went to great lengths to learn everything she could about them. As a writer, it is always good to get inside a character's head. Meyer did just that in order to learn what made Edward tick. "I did try an experiment of rewriting the first chapter from the first-person perspective of Edward, and it was a lot more bloodthirsty coming from the vampire's point of view."[14]

As many authors do, Meyer spent a lot of time thinking about her characters even when she was not at her computer. Listening to music or watching television would conjure up thoughts of certain characters. "As I hear a song begin, I think, 'Ooooh, that's an Edward song,' or 'That's a Jacob song.' When I watch TV now, I think of the actors I see in terms of what characters they could play in my books."[15]

The Cullen family is a coven of vampires that is led by Carlisle and Esme. Their undead group of children includes Edward, Emmett, Jasper, Rosalie, and Alice. Each character has a unique ability or power. "I love the idea of a group of people and all of them can do something really well. They're special, but they're strongest when they work together."[16] Meyer referred to the X-Men as a source of inspiration for the Cullen coven. "I think that really came into play when I was subconsciously forming the Cullen family. Though I certainly wasn't thinking about Cyclops when I was writing about them, I think it was there in the layers underneath."[17]

The Cullen vampires may not have Cyclops to deal with, but they do have a pack of werewolves to contend with. Meyer's werewolves are large and super strong. Together, they can take down a vampire.

Meyer listened to a lot of music while writing *Twilight*. It fueled her muse. Songs by My Chemical Romance were especially helpful when she was creating her main werewolf. "This band is so in touch for me with Jacob's character." She found their song "Famous Last Words" reflected Jacob's romantic side.[18]

Jacob Black and his father, Billy, belong to the Quileute Tribe, and Meyer did do some research on their background and history. "All of the legends in the books are part of their tradition, the werewolves and so on."[19] The Quileute trace the formation of their tribe back hundreds of years ago. Documentation on their Web site states: "According to their ancient creation story, the Quileutes were changed from wolves by a wandering Transformer."[20]

Speaking about the relationship between her vampires and werewolves, Meyer said, "The only legend that is not part of the Quileute tradition is

The comic book superheroes in the X-Men helped inspire the Cullen clan in Meyer's *Twilight* series. "Though I certainly wasn't thinking about Cyclops [the X-Men character, pictured above] when I was writing about them [the Cullen family], I think it was there in the layers underneath," Meyer said.

the part I devised specifically to fit the Cullens."[21] In "Scary Stories," chapter 6 of *Twilight*, fifteen-year-old Jacob explains the lore of his tribe to Bella. "Another legend claims that we descended from wolves—and that the wolves are our brothers still. It's against tribal laws to kill them."[22] He goes on to reveal the stories of the *cold ones*— better known as vampires—and how they are the natural enemy of the wolf. Jacob explains to Bella that his great-grandfather was the tribal elder who made a truce with the cold ones because they were different and did not hunt like other vampires. They were more civilized.

When Bella makes the connection between the Cullen family and the civilized clan of vampires, she asks Jacob, "So how does it fit in with the Cullens? Are they like the cold ones your great-grandfather met?" Meyer skillfully amped up the tension with Jacob's response, "They are the *same* ones."[23]

In the early stages of writing *Twilight*, Meyer listened to a lot of Linkin Park. The beat of their music helped Meyer tap into the action scenes. "'By Myself' was a song I listened to in loops because just the sound of it, and the words of aloneness, the attackers behind you."[24] She was inspired by many other music groups but said, "[M]y biggest muse is the band Muse, ironically enough."[25]

Meyer's writing journey began with a dream so it seems fitting that after she had her novel completed, her nocturnal vampire made another appearance. "I actually did have a dream after *Twilight* was finished of Edward coming to visit me—only I had gotten it wrong and he did drink blood like every other vampire and you couldn't live on animals the way I'd written it. We had this conversation and he was terrifying."[26]

Having the dream that inspired her romantic vampire novel, and then the having another dream when she had finished it, Meyer's creativity had gone full-circle. With her sister cheering her on, it would not be long before Meyer was living her own overnight success story.

Chapter 6

The Making of a Phenomenon

With her novel complete, Meyer decided to listen to her big sister's encouragement and explore the publishing process. "I had to Google," Meyer told Ellen DeGeneres during an appearance on Ellen's talk show. "I had to look up what do you do when you write a book."[1]

That Internet search led Meyer to the Web site of author, Janet Evanovich. Evanovich's site offered Meyer the steps she was looking for on how to turn her manuscript into a book. Besides noting the step-by-step advice, Meyer read through the site's questions and answers section for writers.[2]

From there, Meyer began her agent search and started sending out query letters. "I sent letters out to fifteen and I got, I think, nine rejections, and five no answers." One of the fifteen agents asked Meyer to send the first three chapters of the novel.[3] "I only got one bite, but it was from the "dream on, Stephenie" agency at the top of my list."[4]

The company at the top of her list was Writers House, a literary agency located in Manhattan. Agent Jodi Reamer fell in love with Meyer's story and offered to represent her about a month after reading the entire manuscript. Meyer officially became a client of Writers House in October of 2003—just two months after completing the novel.[5] Although most writers spend years writing and submitting before they find an agent or sell a book, Meyer's success came quickly.

After Jodi Reamer sent Meyer's manuscript out to publishing houses, it only took two weeks for nine editors to express interest in the story. Megan Tingley, editor and head of MT Books at Little, Brown and Company, read Meyer's manuscript while she was on an airplane. She was sucked into the story. "It was the combination of desire and danger that drew me in. I could not put it down and I could not wait for the plane to land so I could sign up the book," Tingley said, remembering her initial enthusiasm for the book. By the time Tingley reached the middle of the story, she knew Meyer's book was going to be a huge hit. "On a gut level, I knew I had a bestseller on my hands when I was halfway through the manuscript."[6]

Tingley contacted Jodi Reamer with an offer to buy the completed manuscript, plus sign Meyer on to write two follow-up books for Little, Brown and Company. The amount of money that Tingley offered for the three-book deal was three hundred thousand dollars.

Negotiating the best contract terms possible is part of what an agent does for his or her clients. Being offered one hundred thousand dollars per book was a fantastic offer, but Reamer must have sensed that Tingley really wanted to acquire the work and would probably pay more.

Reamer contacted Meyer to update her and told her they had an offer for three books. No doubt, Meyer had to be thrilled. Then Reamer informed her that she actually turned down Tingley's offer and had asked for more—a lot

Twilight fans Shar and Travis Petersen with Stephenie Meyer at an "I Love Edward Cullen" party held in Provo, Utah, on February 2, 2007.

more. Reamer made a counter offer and asked for one million dollars. Meyer took the information in and tried to stay calm and professional. "It was the most surreal day," she said. "I almost threw up."[7]

Once negotiations were over, Meyer ended up with a staggering sale. Reamer sold the manuscript to Little, Brown and Company for seven hundred fifty thousand dollars. It was the largest offer the publisher had ever given to an unknown, unpublished author.

"It's been a real whirlwind—more like a lightning strike," Meyer said about her fast and amazing road to publication.[8] It had only been six months time between the writing down her dream to her incredible sale. She understood her good fortune was not the usual path for most authors. She expressed her feelings in a 2005 interview that appeared in *BookPage*. "Sometimes I feel guilty. People go through so much, and I skipped over the bad parts. It feels like cheating, somehow."[9]

The deal with Little, Brown and Company was far more than Meyer ever dreamed of. She had been hoping to get about ten thousand dollars to pay off her minivan.[10] As a car lover from an early age, Meyer spent some of her money and splurged on an Infiniti G35 coupe—a sporty, but luxurious car that any of her car-loving characters would drool over.[11] Her new car came with all the extras, too. "So it's nice to drive something besides the minivan on the rare occasion that I go somewhere without my kids."[12]

In *Twilight*, Bella drives an old 1953 Chevy pickup truck. It is a gift from her father, given to her when she moves back to Forks, Washington, to live with him. When they arrive at their house, Bella spots the truck:

> There, parked on the street in front of the house that never changed, was my new—well, new to me— truck. It was a faded red color, with big rounded fenders and a bulbous cab. To my intense surprise, I loved it.[13]

The Cullens have different tastes when it comes to vehicles, but each car seems well matched to individual characters. Carlisle Cullen drives a Mercedes S55AMG. Rosalie gets around in her BMW M3 convertible, and Emmett travels the roads in his Jeep Wrangler. Edward drives a silver Volvo S60R, but there was another car that Meyer used in *Twilight*, which was cut out during the editing process. Originally, Meyer had Edward escort Bella to the prom in a car that any teen would die for—a flashy Aston Martin V12 Vanquish. The decision to cut that car out of *Twilight* and stick with Edward's Volvo meant Meyer could save that special ride for use in another book.

Cutting the Aston Martin was not the only change that Meyer made to her original draft of the novel. She initially had a more concrete ending but made changes so Bella's and Edward's story could be told through a series of books.[14]

Back when Meyer sent out queries to agents,

the original title for her hefty story was *Forks*. After she signed agreements with Jodi Reamer, changing the title was the first thing the two worked on. "We played around with a lot of different titles, and nothing seemed to convey the right feel. We brainstormed through emails for about a week. The word *twilight* was on a list of 'words with atmosphere' that I sent her. Though these words were meant to be used in combination with something else, the word *twilight* stood out to both of us."[15]

Part of the writing process included writing a first draft, rewriting what was written, and then revising the story again and again. At the revision stage, authors work closely with their editors until the work is ready to go to print.

Not long after *Twilight* was released, Meyer spoke to aspiring authors and other spectators during a visit to Arizona State University in November of 2005. "I do want to make one point about writing; even today, if I turned to any page in the story, I could probably find at least five words I would want to change, so you never really finish; you just find a good place in the process to quit."

> "The word *twilight* stood out to both of us."

The buzz surrounding Meyer's incredible book deal had the publishing industry, booksellers, and readers anticipating *Twilight*'s release. Little, Brown and Company gave *Twilight* a lot of promotion and drew interest in the upcoming book with a publicity blitz. Once it was released, the reviews were favorable. The following review from *School Library Journal* ran in their October 2005 issue in the section listing titles geared toward grades nine and up:

> Headstrong, sun-loving, 17-year-old Bella declines her mom's invitation to move to Florida, and instead reluctantly opts to move to her dad's cabin in the dreary, rainy town of Forks, WA. She becomes intrigued with Edward Cullen, a distant, stylish, and disarmingly handsome senior, who is also a vampire. When he reveals that his specific clan hunts wildlife instead of humans, Bella deduces that she is safe from his blood-sucking instincts and therefore free to fall hopelessly in love with him. The feeling is mutual, and the resulting volatile romance smolders as they attempt to hide Edward's identity from her family and the rest of the school. Meyer adds an eerie new twist to the mismatched, star-crossed lovers theme: predator falls for prey, human falls for vampire. This tension strips away any pretense readers may have about the everyday teen romance novel, and kissing, touching, and talking take on an entirely new meaning when one small mistake could be life-threatening. Bella and Edward's struggle to make their relationship work becomes a struggle for survival, especially when vampires from an outside clan infiltrate the Cullen territory and head straight for her. As a result, the novel's danger-factor skyrockets as the excitement of secret love and hushed affection morphs into a terrifying race to stay alive. Realistic, subtle, succinct, and easy to follow, *Twilight* will have readers dying to sink their teeth into it.[16]

Twilight received starred reviews and was

picked as a *New York Times* Editor's Choice, a *Publishers Weekly* "Best Book of the Year," and a *Teen People* "Hot List" pick. The American Library Association named it one of the "Top Ten Books for Young Adults" and included it in their "Top Ten Books for Reluctant Readers" list. Amazon.com sold copy after copy and named *Twilight* "Best Book of the Decade . . . So Far."

Meyer went on tour to promote her book and her readership grew quickly. Diehard fans went to bookstores to hear her speak and have their copies of *Twilight* signed. In November 2005, Meyer appeared at the Harry W. Schwartz bookstore in Mequon, Wisconsin. Since it was early in the publicity blitz, this event included about a dozen readers. Of those, only three were teenage girls.

Meyer was accompanied by her publicity director,

A tourist visiting Forks, Washington, holds up a sign referencing Meyer's *Twilight* series. Forks, of course, is the fictional location where the *Twilight* characters reside.

Elizabeth Eulberg. Meyer spoke about *Twilight*, answered questions from the audience, and then signed copies of the book. Afterward, Meyer spent about forty-five minutes talking to the three teenagers. "Stephenie was also cool enough to correspond with me by email for several months after we met," one of the teens reported.[17] Meyer had even taken time out of working on her next book in order to correspond. Before she signed her letter, she wrote: "And tomorrow I'm totally working on New Moon! So let it be written, so let it be done!"[18] Meyer was also kind enough to send the teen a copy of a photograph that Eulberg took of them.

After the release of *Twilight*, Meyer was touring and working on other books in the series when she was able. Attendance to Meyer's author appearances was cozy in the beginning. Her sister Emily recalled how it was early in Meyer's career. "It would be me and my five little friends, because of course I loaned out my books and got my whole neighborhood reading, and we'd go to the ice cream store, and she'd read some of the *Midnight Sun* manuscript to us."[19]

While her book was making Meyer a household name, her knack for being so personable at events made her fans love her even more. Plus, she launched a Web site that expanded her popularity to the online community. "Stephenie's fans are rabid," editor Megan Tingley said. "Stephenie has tapped into something very deep in her readers, and they respond on an emotional level. She really

Meyer reads from *Midnight Sun* during an "I Love Edward Cullen" party held in Provo, Utah, on February 2, 2007.

understands the hopes and fears of teenage girls."[20]

Twilight was not just popular with teenage girls, though. Bella and Edward's story attracted readers ranging from tween through adult, female and male. Meyer began writing for her twenty-nine-year-old self so she understood the appeal to readers out of their teens. "I would say that it is probably appropriate for adults and teen readers, but not too young," she said.[21]

The suspense-filled romance has love, fast cars, a vivid setting, and drop-dead gorgeous characters. Meyer talked about being scared of monsters, and she explained why vampires appeal to readers, "Vampires are the only ones who are dangerous, scary, and, at the same time, hot."[22]

The cover of *Twilight* shows two hands—one feminine, one masculine—holding a perfect red apple. On her Web site, Meyer explained how the cover relates to the theme of the story:

> The apple on the cover of *Twilight* represents "forbidden fruit." I used the scripture from Genesis (located just after the table of contents) because I loved the phrase "the fruit of the knowledge of good and evil.". . . To me it says: choice.[23]

Using the apple to symbolize choice has meaning for both Bella and Edward. "I really think that's the underlying metaphor of my vampires," Meyer said. "It doesn't matter where you're stuck in life or what you think you have to do; you can always choose something else. There's always a different path."[24]

Meyer's path in life now included book tours

and publicity, but she was not letting it go to her head. "I think that after thirty years of being the most normal person in the whole world, it's really hard to become ungrounded. When I'm not out on tour or doing photo shoots, I tend to just forget about it all."[25]

By July 2008, *Twilight* had 3.3 million copies in print, including hardcover and paperbacks. It was released in thirty-eight languages and had become a worldwide phenomenon.

Chapter 7

Moon and Stars

*M*eyer continued to write about her characters even after she had completed the *Twilight* manuscript. "I found myself writing multiple epilogues—hundred-plus page epilogues. I quickly realized I wasn't ready to stop writing about Bella and Edward."[1] At that point, Meyer began writing the sequel, *New Moon*. After that, she kept the story line going and eventually ended up writing four books in one year.

While writing *New Moon*, Meyer returned to using music for inspiration. This time around, she listened to a lot of songs by Marjorie Fair. "It's just this heartbreaking music where pain is done so beautifully."[2]

By October 2005, Meyer was in the editing stage of *New Moon*. She compared the process to giving birth. "It's equal in pain, and can drag on and on."[3] During the revision process, Meyer found herself having to make changes to two different versions she had saved on her computer. One version included all twenty-four chapters as a whole and continuous document. The other version was saved as twenty-four separate documents. This created more work and was time consuming for Meyer. "I've been making editorial changes in *both places*. I'm going to have to print both out so I can lay the pages side by side to find the differences and choose the ones I like best."[4]

New Moon includes the same cast of characters as *Twilight*, including Edward, Jacob, and Bella. Jacob's story line is intensified by his transformation into a werewolf. Edward's character is not seen as much because he left Forks for Bella's own good, but his presence is always lurking. For this second book in the *Twilight* saga, Meyer's editor wanted her to beef up Edward's abilities by giving him the power to become invisible.[5] Even though he does not appear in large sections of the book, Meyer kept him fully-formed and decided not to expand his abilities after all.

Meyer introduced a second coven of vampires, the Volturi. The head vampires of this clan included Aro, Caius, and Marcus, and they are thought to be more than three thousand years old. Because of a misunderstanding, Edward believes Bella has died. He is heartbroken and goes to Italy to taunt the Volturi into ending his existence. When Alice and Bella get word of Edward's plans, they fly to

Volterra, Italy, to save Edward. With Edward and Bella reunited, Meyer has them come face to face with the Volturi for some hair-raising scenes.

The dark romance between Bella and Edward has been compared to the forbidden love of William Shakespeare's characters in *Romeo and Juliet*. There are similarities between the plots as well. Both Edward and Romeo move away from their towns, leaving Bella and Juliet desperate to see their loves again. Both female characters take drastic measures to deal with their loss. And in each story, both Edward and Romeo are led to believe that the object of their desire has died.

New Moon also introduced readers to several new modes of transportation. Since Jacob is handy with cars and motorcycles, Meyer gave him a Volkswagen Rabbit to tinker on. He also struck a deal with Bella and fixed up a couple of old motor-cycles for them. He got the Harley Sprint and Bella got the Honda. Meyer spared no expense or style for Alice and has her driving a Porsche 911 Turbo.

New Moon was released in September 2006 with an initial printing of one-hundred thousand copies. Meyer held a book signing and question and answer session at a Barnes and Noble. She talked about her favorite parts of her books. "The meadow scene obviously started it all, so that one will always be really important to me. The scene in Volterra, that scene came very, very freely to me, and that's some of my favorite writing in that scene; it came like a movie to me and I just wrote it down as that scene. I like that a lot." Her fans cheered in agreement.

Meyer's fans adore her and she feels just the same about them. She enjoys their questions and loves how into the stories they are. "You really can't write for a better audience. I say to all other authors: If you're not writing for teenage girls, you're missing out on a lot of love."[6]

During an author visit to Arizona State University, Meyer was asked about her newfound stardom. She said, "I am still very new to giving presentations, signing books, and touring as an author, although I like to visit young readers all over the country and talk about books and read-ing. I still feel mostly like a mom and just 'Stephenie' most of the time."[7]

Meyer toured with her publicity director and thanked her in the acknowledgments of *New Moon*, by writing: "Love, kisses, and gratitude to my publicist, the beautiful Elizabeth, for making my touring experience less a chore and more a pajama party."[8]

Meyer's star status became even brighter when the reviews of *New Moon* started appearing in lit-erary publications. In July 2006, *Kirkus Reviews* had this to say about Meyer's second book:

> All is not well between demon-magnet Bella and Edward Cullen, her vampire Romeo. An innocent papercut at Edward's house puts Bella in grave danger when various members of the Cullen family can barely resist their hunger at the smell of blood. The Cullens promptly leave town, afraid of endan-gering Edward's beloved, and Bella sinks into an

Meyer signs copies of her books during an appearance in Cologne, Germany.

overwhelming depression. Months later, she finally emerges from her funk to rebuild her life, focusing on her friendship with besotted teen Jacob from the reservation. Bella's unhealthy enthrallment to Edward leads her into dangerous and self-destructive behavior despite her new friends, and supernatural complications are bound to reappear. . . . Psychic miscommunications and angst-ridden dramatic gestures lead to an exciting page-turner of a conclusion drenched in the best of Gothic romantic excess. Despite Bella's flat and obsessive personality, this tale of tortured demon lovers entices.

Bella's personality and character traits have been scrutinized ever since *Twilight* made its debut. She has been called insecure, whiny, and self-destructive. Most fictional characters have flaws and Bella is no different. They are there as internal obstacles that Bella must learn from, overcome, or embrace. They are part of her character growth.

Meyer's young adult audience obviously sees something in Bella they can relate to. Maybe they sympathize with Bella's broken family, or they understand her angst about loving someone who is an outsider. It could be that fans simply enjoy rooting for a normal teenage girl who has found herself between rival vampires and werewolves. Whatever their personal reason may be, readers have sunk their teeth into Meyer's series.

Readers were not the only ones to latch onto Bella's story. In July 2007—one year before *Twilight* racked up the enormous 3.3 million in sales numbers—Meyer gave her online fans a news update that they had been anxiously waiting for.

Summit Entertainment had optioned *Twilight* and plans were in the works to bring the story to the big screen.

The rights to the movie had actually been acquired before the novel was even released. In 2004, MTV and Maverick Films had teamed up to negotiate making a feature film of the novel. Speaking about her surprise over the fact that she had a three-book deal and movie deal, Meyer said, "It felt very strange, like some sort of practical joke."[9]

Then, in April 2007, MTV's time to finalize the movie deal lapsed. Meyer and her agent began talking to other production companies. Summit Entertainment swooped in and took MTV's place.

Meyer also contributed to an anthology that came out in April 2007. *Prom Nights From Hell* is a collection of short stories written by several well-known authors. *Booklist* wrote that "a prom is nearly destroyed by warring biblical demons; then dreamy half-angel Gabe comes to the rescue" to describe Meyer's story, *Hell on Earth*.

On May 5, 2007, Meyer threw a huge prom at Arizona State University. The gym was transformed with red and black decorations. Hundreds of teenagers and young women attended wearing formal prom dresses. Meyer wore a deep red gown, adorned with rhinestones and beads. Except for a braid wrapped around her crown, her long, dark hair flowed over her shoulders.

The idea to hold the prom came from some fans who told Meyer that they planned to dress up and hold a prom party the next time she was in their town. Meyer and her publicist loved the idea so much that they decided to host the event.[10]

They scheduled the prom around the release of a special edition of *New Moon*, and the upcoming release of Meyer's third book, *Eclipse*. The special edition of *New Moon* included temporary tattoos, a poster of *Eclipse*, and its opening chapter. At the event, Meyer read the first chapter of *Eclipse* to her party guests. She signed more than one thousand books by the time the line of fans had stopped.

This time around, Meyer's prom was a full-blown publicity event for her books and fans. Twihards— as her fans are known as—came from all over the world to attend. They formed committees and helped with planning and decorations. One can only imagine the type of car Meyer arrived in for this prom. With hundreds of camera-ready fans and publicity staff, there was definitely no shortage of photo opportunities.

Stephenie Meyer signs a copy of *Twilight* for a fan during the promotional "prom" that took place at Arizona State University on May 5, 2007.

The popularity of Meyer and her *Twilight* saga had Little, Brown and Company expecting huge sales for *Eclipse*. They released the third book in August 2007 with an initial print run of one million copies. *Eclipse* bumped *Harry Potter and the Deathly Hallows* from its spot at the top of the sales charts. Meyer had become a multimillionaire in less than four years.

When reviews of *Eclipse* hit the media, the write-ups were mostly positive. There was the occasional snarky comment about Meyer's use of adverbs. Reviewers' personal opinions about Bella's dramatic flare sometimes appeared in reviews, too. Hopefully, Meyer was made aware of the fact that J. K. Rowling also had her use of adverbs brought up in reviews. Overall, reviewers understood the heart and soul of Meyer's book.

A review in *People* magazine said: "For a huge subset of teen (and some of their elders), the most eagerly awaited book of the season isn't about Harry but Edward, the impossibly handsome hero of Meyer's bestselling series about a coven of elegant, conscientious vampires in Washington state. . . . Meyer's plots are melodramatic, but her writing has a hypnotic quality that puts the readers right inside the dense, rainy thickets of the Olympic peninsula where her vampires and werewolves square off."[11]

With Edward and Jacob teaming up to protect Bella from evil vampires in *Eclipse*, fan frenzy escalated. Diehard Twihards had split and created Team Edward and Team Jacob. Bella remained all about Edward, becoming an immortal being and joining him as his vampire wife for eternity.

Good versus evil is a recurring theme in *Eclipse* and Bella is the center of attention of both the vampires and the werewolves. The issue of pre-marital sex is strong in this installment of the saga when Meyer heightens Bella's sexual desires. A deeper romantic tension is felt between the love-struck duo and, at times, the reader is left breathless.

Publishers Weekly wrote about Meyer's keen ability to tap into teen angst and young love: "The supernatural elements accentuate the ordinary human dramas of growing up. Jake and Edward's competition for Bella feels particularly authentic, especially in their apparent desire to best each other as much as to win Bella. Once again the author presents teenage love as an almost inhuman force."[12]

When the summer of 2007 came to an end, Meyer's family life and daily routines changed. She suddenly found herself with extra chunks of writing time. The Meyer boys were at an age where they needed a little less attention from their mom. They were becoming a bit more independent. "For the first time this fall, I'll have all three of my kids in all-day school. So that's just going to be an amazing amount of time, I can barely compute it."[13]

Chapter 8

Aliens, Vampires, and Fan Frenzy

Before the final installment of the *Twilight* saga became available to the public, Little, Brown and Company released Meyer's first novel aimed at adult readers. *The Host* is a paranormal romance set in the future. Meyer describes it as "science fiction for people who don't like science fiction."

The idea for *The Host* came to Meyer during a long drive through the Arizona desert. "I have no idea what sparked the strange foundation of a body-snatching alien in love with the host body's boyfriend. . . . I could tell there was something compelling in the idea of such a complicated triangle."[1]

Meyer used a notebook to write an outline for her novel idea and then deepened the story once she was able to get to her computer. As with *Twilight*, Meyer began writing *The Host* for her own entertainment. It soon became something she could not stay away from and it blossomed into more than a side project.[2]

When the manuscript of *The Host* went up for auction, it sold for six hundred thousand dollars. Money aside, Meyer was thrilled about the sale because it allowed her expand her readership and prove she was more than "just a vampire girl."[3]

The Host came out in May of 2008 to a flurry of sales. The publisher had anticipated a lot of interest and set the first printing at five hundred thousand copies. Their instincts and expectations were right. *The Host* debuted at number one on the best-seller lists.

> *The Host* debuted at number one on the best-seller lists.

Reviews of Meyer's newest work were affirming. *Library Journal* praised her first adult novel saying: "It lives up to the hype, blending science fiction and romance in a way that has never worked so well. In this page-turner, Meyer explores what happens to relationships when two beings inhabit the same physical body."[4]

A reviewer for *USA Today* wrote: "Unlike the classic human-vs-alien stories in which ghastly looking creatures (think *Alien*) are the norm, Meyer offers aliens so docile you wonder how they manage to take over the Earth. Still, the effect is frightening."[5]

Speaking about her alien love story, Meyer said, "It's definitely a departure in that it's a whole new cast and crew in my head. . . . I think my established readers will be comfortable with it; they'll get into the rhythm of it and find it sounds like me."[6]

Even though *The Host* has some gritty and frightening scenes, there is nothing particularly graphic it in. It appeals to both adult and teen readers, mainly because of its love story. Meyer said that aspect of the story is one of her favorite things. "Getting to explore love from so many different angles. Love for community, for self, for family—romantic love and platonic love."[7]

Meyer definitely has a knack for writing novels about love. Whether they involve vampires, werewolves, or aliens, all of her novels are dripping with romance. During an author visit to promote *The Host*, a fan asked Meyer where her love stories come from. Meyer explained that the intensity of the love she has for her children is the springboard for the emotion in her writing. She also said that "one of the things that I find really enjoyable to explore is the idea of love. I like looking at my own life and my friends and family and how love changes who you are. It fascinates me."[8]

The time that Meyer was used to spending as a stay-at-home mom was now used more and more for book promotion and tours. Her busy schedule took her away from her home and family and sometimes interfered with family events. Meyer was on tour during her son's kindergarten graduation, but like many busy families, one parent was present. Her husband had left his job at an accounting firm in order to stay at home with their children and attend to their daily needs while Meyer was working.

Once her ten-city book tour for *The Host* ended, Meyer began preparing for the release of her most anticipated romance novel, *Breaking Dawn*. Editor Megan Tingley summed up Little, Brown and Company's excitement by saying, "Stephenie Meyer has written a dazzling grand finale to an epic story. And with the extraordinary excitement surrounding the publication of *Breaking Dawn*, I'm thrilled that legions of new readers will now discover the saga that has already captivated millions around the world."[9]

A bookstore banner promotes the upcoming release of *Breaking Dawn* in the summer of 2008.

Breaking Dawn was released just three months after *The Host*. It was the end of one saga and a beginning for another. The summer of 2008 was a whirlwind of promotion and tours. Releasing two books in a year is an amazing accomplishment, and Meyer's success was recognized by David Young, chairman and chief executive officer of Hachette Book Group USA. "Stephenie Meyer has already achieved so much in her young career and this year further establishes her as a major force in the publishing industry."[10]

A media and publicity blitz was planned to promote *Breaking Dawn*. Parties were held all over the United States in anticipation of the midnight release on August 2, 2008. Bookstores stayed open past usual hours to allow buyers to join the festivities before the 12:01 release. Bookstore partygoers were treated to *Twilight* saga chocolate, *Breaking Dawn* stickers, scavenger hunts, fang painting, and look-alike contests.

Little, Brown and Company prepared for blockbuster sales by printing 3.2 million copies as a first run. A report in *Publishers Weekly* announced that *Breaking Dawn* had sold 1.3 million copies on its first publication day. Those numbers were the largest single-day sales in the history of Little, Brown and Company.[11] The four hundred thousand dollars they paid Meyer for the fourth book was earned back with record sales.

Instead of promoting the final book with typical author visits and book signings, Meyer traveled to four major cities for her *Breaking Dawn Concert Series* tour. Justin Furstenfeld of the band, Blue October, toured with her. Their first stop was the Nokia Theater in New York where she entertained about two thousand fans at the sold-out event. Fans that could not attend the event were able to watch it live via *Entertainment Weekly*'s Web site. It was estimated that more than two hundred fifty thousand viewers watched the streaming video. After New York, the tour moved on to Chicago, Los Angeles, and Seattle.

Whether they call themselves Twihards, Twilighters, or Fanpires, the events drew huge crowds of enthusiastic fans. Some had made posters, many wore homemade T-shirts identifying them as "Team Edward" or "Team Jacob," and a few fans even wore red contacts.

During the concert, Meyer spoke about the lyrics that inspired her writing and Justin Furstenfeld sang several songs for the crowd. Having Justin be part of her tour was exciting for Meyer. "Music played a major role in the writing of the *Twilight* Saga and [it's] thrilling to be able to incorporate my love of music into these special events for my readers. I'm a huge Blue October fan! To have Justin at these *Breaking Dawn* events playing songs that inspired scenes in the book is cooler than anything I could have imagined."[12]

Breaking Dawn is 754 pages long, making it the heftiest volume in the *Twilight* series. It had been longer, but Meyer cut about eighty pages during editing. The entire four-book saga is more than twenty-four hundred pages. Meyer had originally planned for the saga to be told in three books but realized that would not be enough. "When you create a world like that—when you create Edward and Bella—if you stop writing, it's like you're killing them. I couldn't do that. I had to let them go on and see what was going to happen."[13]

As readers of the first three books expected,

Twilight fans could not wait to get their hands on *Breaking Dawn* when it was released on August 2, 2008.

Breaking Dawn starts with the wedding of Bella and Edward. It is a traditional wedding—with flowers, music, lavish decorations, and an arch to say their vows under. The words, "As long as we both shall live," take on a whole new meaning for the couple who are about to spend eternity together.

In order to keep the public from learning the ending of the saga before the actual book release, Little, Brown and Company decided not to send advance copies out to reviewers. Once the reviews hit the media, they were mixed. *School Library Journal* had this to say about *Breaking Dawn*:

> The story opens with Bella and Edward's wedding, and relations between Jacob and Bella remain uneasy. On honeymoon and unshackled from any further concerns about premarital sex, Edward fulfills his promise to consummate their marriage before he changes Bella into a vampire. An unexpected conception throws their idyllic world back into chaos as factions (both wolf and vampire) battle over whether or not to destroy the potential monster that is killing Bella from within. The captivating angst, passions, and problems manage to satisfyingly fill pages where surprisingly little action takes place, even after the powerful child's birth brings the Cullen family under the scrutiny of the Volturi. . . . While darker and more mature than the previous titles, Meyer's twists and turns are not out of character. Fans may distress as the happy ending for everyone, including a girl for Jacob, lessens the importance and pain of tough decisions and difficult self-sacrifices that caused great grief in previous books, but they will flock to it and enjoy it nonetheless.[14]

Meyer knew *Breaking Dawn* was more intense than the first three books. At the request of her editors, she toned down some of the violence for the final product. At one point, there was even a discussion about having a rating of some sort on the book. "It was for an age limit of fifteen or sixteen and a warning. I think the content is just a little harder to handle, a little bit more grown-up for really young kids. I have nine-year-old readers, and I think it's too old for them. Some of it's violence, and some of it's just mature themes."[15]

> **"I think the content is just a little harder to handle, a little bit more grown-up . . ."**

Meyer also knew that some fans would be disappointed with the way she ended the saga. She was the only one who could complete the story, even though readers had their own ideas of how the saga could end. Shortly after the release of *Breaking Dawn*, readers began commenting and expressing their love or dissatisfaction with the book. Many unhappy buyers went as far as to return their books. Just as they had done for Team Edward and Team Jacob, Meyer's fans had split into sides.

Meyer was understandably shook up even though there were millions of fans cheering for *Breaking Dawn*. "It's been hard. The book did so

Though there was some negative criticism, most *Twilight* fans were pleased with *Breaking Dawn* and the resolution it brought to the series.

much better than I thought it would. . . . And then the negative reaction was so much more than I was expecting."[16]

After the bad press settled down, Meyer realized that no matter how her story had ended or what happened to her characters, she would not be able to make everyone happy. She wrote the stories as she saw them and had to be happy with that achievement and move forward.

Meyer's diehard fans rallied together and created Team Stephenie to support her. While they anxiously waited for the movie version of *Twilight* to be released, fans in Forks, Washington, kept the frenzy going. The town made September 13 Stephenie Meyer Day and celebrated Bella's birthday with a party.

Chapter 9

Lightning Strikes and Red Carpets

Because of her enormous fan following and fast rise to fame, Meyer's career has often been compared to that of J. K. Rowling, creator of Harry Potter. Both authors were struck by a story premise that would not leave them alone. While Meyer's characters came to her in a dream, it has been said that Rowling's idea came to her while she was on a train in England. The Harry Potter storyline simply popped into her head.

Meyer gives Rowling credit for helping to create a place for long books for children. "If it weren't for J. K. Rowling, I think publishers wouldn't be willing to put out lengthy books. It just proves that if a book is good enough, young people will read it."[1]

Being compared to Rowling is a major

compliment, but it also puts a lot of pressure on Meyer. "There will never be another J. K. Rowling. . . . I'm just happy being Stephenie Meyer. That's cool enough for me."[2]

Meyer has been an inspiration to authors and aspiring writers, too. Her journey has encouraged others to try to break into publishing. Her successful vampire romances have also helped make paranormal books very popular with readers of all ages.

Speaking about her path to publication, Meyer said: "Sometimes I feel a little bit like an ambassador for people who want to write because I represent how lucky you can get. For most people it's a really difficult journey—being published, writing your first book, getting out there. For me it's been like a lightning strike, where I went from being a stay-at-home mom to all of a sudden, without much effort on my part, being a stay-at-home mom who also has a really great career writing. I like to tell people that it can happen."[3]

A famous quote that states, "The harder I work, the luckier I get," would be a perfect motto for Meyer because she clearly worked hard and wrote a lot. It was her story, her commitment to writing, and her decision to pursue publication that started it all. Her journey to success was extremely fast, but it was her talent and skill that made the path a smooth one.

By the time Meyer's *Breaking Dawn Concert Series* ended, she had spent many hours on the road. She had spoken to thousands of fans and appeared on several television and news shows. She talked about *Breaking Dawn*, her fans reactions, and future projects. It was time for her to move forward and gear up for the next media blitz for the movie *Twilight*. She had about three months between the *Breaking Dawn Concert Series* and the *Twilight* premiere.

What should have been a time of celebration and relaxation was dampened when she received some disturbing news. Pages of an unfinished manuscript she was working on had been leaked and posted on the Internet. *Midnight Sun* was a work in progress and there had been plans to release it as the final installment of the *Twilight* series.

"There will never be another J. K. Rowling. . . . I'm just happy being Stephenie Meyer."

Meyer was rightfully upset that her work was made available to the public without her consent. On August 2008, she posted a message to her fans on her Web site. "My partial draft of *Midnight Sun* was illegally posted on the Internet and has since been virally distributed without my knowledge or permission or the knowledge or permission of my publisher."[4]

Meyer had given a few copies of her draft to people she trusted and was able to identify which

Stephenie Meyer on the red carpet prior to the premiere of the film adaptation of *Twilight* in Los Angeles on Monday, November 17, 2008.

copy it was that was posted online. The leak of her work onto the World Wide Web distressed her, but she did not believe it was done with "malicious intent." Meyer used the unfortunate event to give her online readers a brief lesson about copyright and artistic control. "Just because someone buys a book or movie or song, or gets a download off the Internet, doesn't mean that they own the right to reproduce and distribute it. . . . No matter how this is done, it is still dishonest."[5]

Meyer also stated, "I did not want my readers to experience *Midnight Sun* before it was completed, edited and published. I think it is important for everybody to understand that what happened was a huge violation of my rights as an author, not to mention me as a human being."[6]

The draft that was leaked was incomplete and in the beginning stage of writing. According to Meyer, "the writing is messy and flawed and full of mistakes." The initial distribution of the work in progress was out of Meyer's control. Once word got out that *Midnight Sun* was available, fans had to decide between reading the illegal posting and being loyal to their favorite author.

Meyer made the decision to regain control of her work and posted it on her Web site for everyone to read freely. "I've decided to make the draft available here. This way, my readers don't have to feel they have to make a sacrifice to stay honest." Putting the unfinished manuscript on her Web site was a brave and unselfish gesture, but Meyer was discouraged by events. "I feel too sad about what has happened to continue working on *Midnight Sun*, and so it is on hold indefinitely."[7] Fans were saddened by the news as well and some began petitions supporting Meyer and urging her to complete *Midnight Sun* and release it in book form.

It was actually Meyer's fans that inspired her to write *Midnight Sun* in the first place. She had heard that fans were writing fiction about *Twilight* and posting it online it for other fans to read. Meyer read some of the fan fiction and said, "It ranged from really good to really silly, but one thing all the stories had in common was that they weren't getting Edward right."[8] Meyer began thinking about how the story would be told using Edward's point of view. She was intrigued by the idea and eventually made time to sit down and let Edward's version flow.

The leaked draft that Meyer eventually posted on her Web site gives readers a better idea of Edward's character and offers a more intense side to the story. For now, fans will have to be satisfied with the online version of *Midnight Sun*. Only time will tell if it will ever join the *Twilight* saga in bookstores.

Meyer had expended a lot of energy dealing with the *Midnight Sun* mess right after being on back-to-back book tours. After going through some difficult times, she took some time for herself, worked on other projects, and spent extra time with her family. She also needed to get ready for the upcoming movie release.

By late fall, sales numbers for *Breaking Dawn*

climbed to close to three million copies, and it earned a secure place in the publishing world. The media outlets began to shift their focus and reported more about the hugely anticipated release of *Twilight*.

The buzz about the movie began as soon as it was officially announced that the book would be adapted for the screen. Fans and media followed the moviemaking progress and savored every detail. When Catherine Hardwicke was brought on as director of the film, she was enthusiastic. "When I started reading the book, *Twilight*, I just got swept away into the feeling of this whole, almost obsessive love. A really cool teenager, just falling madly in love, so in love with this guy that she would actually turn into a vampire to be with him. . . . Stephenie really caught the spirit of being a teenager and of your first love."[9]

The on-screen role of Bella Swan was brought to life by actress Kristen Stewart. Stewart had not read or even heard of the *Twilight* books before seeing the script for the movie. She was quickly taken in by the characters and the romance. "Everything I like about the story is so basic. It's about what drives you to love."[10]

Stewart's stunning, yet ordinary appearance matches the description of her character very well. She fits the part of dark-haired beauty, Bella. When she was cast, Meyer's online fans voiced their approval and so did Meyer. "She's an amazing actress with experience all across the board—action, horror, comedy, romance."[11]

The film poster for *Twilight*, featuring Kristen Stewart as Bella and Robert Pattinson as Edward.

Actor Robert Pattinson was cast for the role of steamy vampire Edward Cullen. Pattinson's chiseled jaw line and piercing eyes were not enough to win fans over right off the bat. Online forums lit up with critical comments from disappointed *Twilight*ers. That was a bit intimidating for Pattinson, but it also made him prepare even harder. He kept to himself, and away from the online message boards, and focused on becoming Edward. He shut himself in as a way to get in tune with his character and even wrote in a journal using Edward's point of view.[12]

Meyer was thrilled with the decision to cast Robert Pattinson from the moment he was chosen to play the leading man. When she looked him up, he seemed to be the vampire of her dreams. "He's definitely got that vampire thing going on,"[13] was the first thing she thought of when she saw him. "And then, when I was on set and I got to watch him go from being Rob to shifting into being Edward, and he actually looked like the Edward in my head, it was a really bizarre experience. It was kind of surreal and almost a little scary. He really had it nailed. So, that was an amazing thing for me."[14]

To complete the paranormal love triangle, actor Taylor Lautner was cast as Jacob Black. His thick, dark hair and handsome boyish looks parallel his *Twilight* character. Lautner spoke about how the movie version would appeal to both genders, not just teen girls. "What we tried to do with the film is add a little more action and horror to it. So now it's for everyone."[15]

During the filming of *Twilight*, Meyer requested that one of the crucial scenes be toned down a bit. In her opinion, Edward and Bella's kissing scene did not need to be so intense. Plus, she wanted to save some of the romantic intensity for possible movie sequels. "The problem is if you're going to continue with the other movies, there's a very gradual build to their physical relationship."[16] The movie executives agreed and reshot the kiss scene.

Another small change Meyer requested had to do with her cameo appearance in the film. She plays a character in a diner, and, originally, the director wanted her to have a line of dialogue in her scene. Meyer did not want her one line distracting from the overall film. So instead of her character ordering a vegetarian plate as planned, she is simply served one.

Much to the delight of Meyer's fans, *Twilight* opened in theaters with a special midnight time slot. Box offices all across the country sold out days before the showing. When Twilighters lined up in droves at more than one thousand movie theaters, they helped *Twilight* take a serious bite out of its competition.

During its opening weekend, *Twilight* brought in more than seventy million dollars. For a movie that cost about thirty million to make and another thirty million to promote, it had made a profit and exceeded the expectations of executives.[17]

The dramatic kiss scene from *Twilight*.

With several more months of big-screen ticket sales, and future DVD sales on top of that, *Twilight* had proven to be another success for Meyer and her *Twilight* franchise.

Meyer attended the red carpet Hollywood premiere of *Twilight* with her family and was very pleased with the movie. "I don't think any other author has had a more positive experience with the makers of her movie adaptation than I have had."[18] Meyer was also happy with the performance of the actors and how they portrayed Bella, Edward, Jacob, and the rest of her characters. She spoke about how the *Twilight*ers had a change of heart over Pattinson being cast as Edward. "I think everybody warmed up pretty fast. Some of it's that

British thing, his charmingness, and some of it's that he's drop dead gorgeous."[19]

The day after *Twilight*'s successful countrywide opening, Summit Entertainment announced plans to bring *New Moon* to the big screen. Fans can look forward to following Bella, Edward, and Jacob as *New Moon* continues the *Twilight* saga. The possibility that the remaining books in Meyer's series will also be adapted for the big screen is very favorable.

Until then, Meyer continues to work on sequels to *The Host* in addition to completing a ghost story, titled *Summer House*.[20] Meyer does not seem to be at a loss for ideas, a fact proven when she reported that she is also writing a novel involving mermaids.[21]

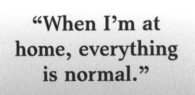

"When I'm at home, everything is normal."

Meyer has not let all of her success go to her head. Even after being named one of *Time* magazine's 100 Most Influential People, she has stayed true to her upbringing. "It is a real separation. When I'm at home, everything is normal. I'm mom. . . . [E]very day is kind of what you expect, very normal and standard, and every now and then I have to be Stephenie Meyer and go on the road and have cameras pointed at me, but generally I get to just be me. It's cool."[22]

It is hard to imagine such a prolific author having time for herself, but Meyer manages to find some downtime to relax. She enjoys watching the Home and Garden Television channel and is a big fan of home improvement shows. Being home for Meyer probably means having the best of both worlds. She is able to be with her family and make a living writing.

It is something she is extremely grateful for. "I am continually shocked by the success of my books. I never take it for granted, and do not count on it in my expectations of my future. It's a very enjoyable thing, and I'll have fun with it while it lasts."[23]

With millions of fans around the globe, it is a good bet that Meyer's success will continue to last for years to come. Her career has taken the book and movie business by storm. She is inspiring to teens and writers alike and has created a life that most people can only dream of.

In Her Own Words

The following section is derived from several Web and print sources containing interviews with Stephenie Meyer conducted between 2007 and 2008.

On the success of the Twilight series:

"I didn't realize the books would appeal to people so broadly. I think some of it's because Bella is an everygirl. She's not a hero, and she doesn't know the difference between Prada and whatever else is out there. She doesn't always have to be cool, or wear the coolest clothes ever. She's normal. And there aren't a lot of girls in literature that are normal. Another thing is that Bella's a good girl, which is sort of how I imagine teenagers, because that's how my teenage years were."[1]

"There's nothing better than getting to live in your world that you've created. And that other people believe in it too."[2]

On creating characters:

"Every now and then there will be a character that is a combination of people I knew—some of the girls in Bella's high school definitely reflect people I knew at that stage in my life—but for the most part, they come out of nowhere. It's amazing, some of the characters are so completely rounded and as soon as I think of them, I know everything about them. And then there are others that I have to work for a little bit harder, and sort of get down to their motivations. A few of them— Rosalie, for example—were difficult. It took me a while to figure out what her thing was."[3]

"[W]hen I write, I forget that it's not real. I'm living the story, and I think people can read that sincerity about the characters. They are real to me while I'm writing them, and I think that makes them real to the readers as well."[4]

"I am constantly surprised by my characters when I write—it's really one of my favorite parts. When a character refuses to do what I had planned for him or her, that's when I know that character is really alive. There were several characters who caught me off guard with *The Host*. One in particular was slated for a bit part as the wingman to the villain. Somehow, he knew he was more than that, and I couldn't stop him from morphing into a main love interest."[5]

Advice for aspiring authors:

"Here's a tip that really helped me with book two and three: forget writing in order. With *New Moon* and *Eclipse*, I wrote out whichever scenes I was interested in, rather than starting at the beginning and working through to the end. I wrote most of the books in scenes, and then went back later and tied the scenes together. It cut out a lot of writer's block to write whatever part I was most interested in at the time. And it makes it easy to finish. By the time you get around to writing the less exciting transitions, expositions, and descriptions, you already have so much done! You can see a full novel coming together, and that's very motivating. (But you really need an outline to work that way—to keep from getting lost!)"[6]

"If you love to write, then write. Don't let your goal be having a novel published, let your goal be enjoying your stories. However, if you finish your story and you want to share it, be brave about it. Don't doubt your story's appeal. If you are a good reader, and you know what is interesting, and your story is interesting to you, then trust in that. If I would have realized that the stories in my head would be as intriguing to others as they were to me, I would probably have started writing sooner. Believe in your own taste."[7]

On the reactions from her fans:

"You know, it's been a gradual building. When I first started doing this, I remember my first event because we were so lucky to scrape together 20 people who would come and listen to someone who had never done a book before. And, that was actually great. We could sit and talk about everything and really get into the characters. I kind of miss those days. We got up to a hundred people and I'd freak out and say, 'There's 100 people in there!' Now, I just have to suck it up and talk to 6,000 people. It's just part of the job, I guess."[8]

"It's really exciting that they care so much about the characters too, because that's how I feel when I'm writing it. I want to know what happens next. I want to see how it develops and what they say to each other, and to have other people feel the same way, it's so gratifying."[9]

Chronology

1973—Stephenie Morgan is born in Hartford, Connecticut.

1978—The Morgan family moves to Phoenix, Arizona.

1992—Stephenie graduates from Chaparral High School.

1994—Marries Christian "Pancho" Meyer.

1997—Graduates from Brigham Young University with a degree in English Literature.

2002—Meyer is a stay-at-home mom of three boys; she engages in activities with her children and is active in her church.

2003—Meyer has the dream that changes her life; she signs an author agreement with her literary agent.

2005—*Twilight* is released with a first printing of seventy-five thousand.

2006—Meyer presents at the National Book Festival in Washington, D.C.; *New Moon* is released with a one hundred thousand first printing.

2007—*Prom Nights From Hell* is released; *Eclipse* is released with a printing of one million copies.

2008—*The Host* is released; *Breaking Dawn* is released with a printing of 3.2 million copies; The *Twilight* movie opens in theaters; Summit Entertainment announces plans to bring *New Moon* to the big screen.

Chapter Notes

Chapter 1. Dreams and Confessions

1. Lev Grossman, "Stephenie Meyer: A New J. K. Rowling?" April 24, 2008, <http://www.time.com/time/magazine/article/0,9171,1734838-1,00.html> (January 15, 2008).

2. Stephenie Meyer, *Twilight* (New York: Little, Brown Books for Young Readers, 2005), p. 274.

3. Stephenie Meyer, "*Twilight* Began as a Very. . ,'" 2005, <http://hachettebookgroupusa.com/Stephenie_Meyer_(1070099)_Article(1).htm> (September 23, 2008).

4. James Blasingame, "Interview With Stephenie Meyer," *Journal of Adolescent and Adult Literacy*, vol. 49, no. 7, April 2006, p 632.

5. Cynthia Leitch Smith, "Author Interview: Stephenie Meyer on *Twilight*," March 27, 2006, <http://cynthialeitichsmith.blogspot.com/2006/03/author-interview-stephenie-meyer-on.html> (August 7, 2008).

6. Ibid.

7. Meyer, "*Twilight* Began as a Very . . ."

8. Ibid.

9. Ibid.

10. Smith.

11. Linda M. Castellitto, "Dream of High School Vampires Inspire a Toothsome Debut," *BookPage*, October 2005, <http://www. bookpage.com/0510bp/stephenie_meyer. html> (August 7, 2008).

12. Rick Margolis, "Love at First Bite," *School Library Journal*, vol. 51, no. 10, p. 37.

13. Meyer.

14. John Mark Eberhart, "Stephenie Meyer's Vampire Novels Were the Dawning of a Career," *Kansas City Star*, May 7, 2008, Newspaper Source, EBSCOhost (January 15, 2009).

15. The Ellen DeGeneres Show interview, Warner Bros. Studio, September 17, 2008.

Chapter 2. "Here's The Story . . ."

1. Megan Irwin, "Charmed, Stephenie Meyer's Vampire Romance Novels Made a Mormon Mom an International Sensation," *Phoenix New Times*, July 12, 2007, <http://www. phoenixnewtimes.com/content/printVersion/ 481142> (November 19, 2008).

2. Ibid.

3. Ibid.

4. Stephenie Meyer, "Unofficial Bio," *StephenieMeyer.com*, n.d., <http://www. stepheniemeyer.com/bio_unofficial.html> (September 22, 2008).

5. Ibid.

6. Cynthia Leitich Smith, "Author Interview: Stephenie Meyer on Twilight," March 27, 2006, <http:cynthialeitichsmith.blogspot. com/2006/03/author-interview-stephenie-meyer-on-html> (August 7, 2008).

7. Meyer, "Unofficial Bio."

8. Stephenie Meyer, e-mail to Sarah Moglia, November 10, 2005.

9. Ibid.

10. Lev Grossman, "Stephenie Meyer: A New J. K. Rowling?" April 24, 2008, <http://www. time.com/time/magazine/article/0,9171, 1734838-2,00.html> (January 15, 2008).

11. "August Feature Article: Bookstories Interview With Stephenie Meyer," August 2006, <http:// chbookstore.qwestoffice.net/fa2006-08.html> (September 22, 2008).

12. Gregory Kirschling, "Stephenie Meyer's 'Twilight' Zone," *EW.com*, August 2, 2008, <http://www.ew.com/ew/article/0,, 20049578,00.html> (September 22, 2008).

13. Michael Brisco, "Could This Be Edward?" September 30, 2008, <http://temparoo. blogspot.com> (November 19, 2008).

14. Author interview with Kemery Judd, December 30, 2008.

15. Shannon Hale, "Squeetus Exclusive: Stephenie Meyer," *Squeetus*, September 8, 2007, <http://oinks.squeetus.com/squeetus exclusives/page/2/> (October 8, 2008).

16. John Mark Eberhart, "Stephenie Meyer's Vampire Novels Were the Dawning of a Career," *Kansas City Star*, May 7, 2008, Newspaper Source, EBSCOhost (January 15, 2009).

17. Kirschling.

18. Karen Valby, "Stephenie Meyer: 12 of My 'Twilight' Inspirations," *EW.com*, November 5, 2008, <http://www.ew.com/ew/gallery/0,,20237747,00.html?print> (November 9, 2008).

19. Ibid.

20. "August Feature Article: Bookstories Interview With Stephenie Meyer."

Chapter 3. Literature and Love

1. Stephenie Meyer, "Unofficial Bio," *StephenieMeyer.com*, n.d., <http://www.stepheniemeyer.com/bio_unofficial.html> (September 22, 2008).

2. John Mark Eberhart, "Stephenie Meyer's Vampire Novels Were the Dawning of a Career," *Kansas City Star*, May 7, 2008, Newspaper Source, EBSCOhost (January 15, 2009).

3. Stephenie Meyer, "Stephenie Meyer Q&A with TMs- Part 1 from 12/28/07," *Twilightmomsforum*, December 28, 2007, <http://twilightmomsforum.freeforums.org/stephenie-meyer-q-a-with-tms-part-1-from-12-28-07-t3222.html> (November 19, 2008).

4. Megan Irwin, "Charmed: Stephenie Meyer's Vampire Romance Novels Made a Mormon Mom an International Sensation," *Phoenix New Times*, July 12, 2007, <http://www.phoenixnewtimes.com/2007-07-12/news/charmed/> (November 19, 2008).

5. Meyer, "Unofficial Bio."

6. Irwin.

7. Karen Valby, "The Vampire Empire," *Entertainment Weekly*, July 18, 2008, p. 25.

8. Irwin.

9. Gregory Kirschling, "Stephenie Meyer's 'Twilight' Zone," *EW.com*, August 2, 2008, <http://www.ew.com/ew/article/0,,20049578,00.html> (September 22, 2008).

Chapter 4. Supermom

1. Lev Grossman, "The Next J. K. Rowling?" *Time*, vol. 171, no. 18, May 5, 2008, p. 49.

2. John Mark Eberhart, "Stephenie Meyer's Vampire Novels Were the Dawning of a Career," *Kansas City Star*, May 7, 2008, Newspaper Source, EBSCOhost (January 15, 2009).

3. Ibid.

4. Megan Irwin, "Charmed: Stephenie Meyer's Vampire Romance Novels Made a Mormon Mom an International Sensation," *Phoenix New Times*, July 12, 2007, <http://www.phoenixnewtimes.com/2007-07-12/news/charmed/> (November 19, 2008).

5. "August Feature Article: Bookstories Interview With Stephenie Meyer," August 2006, <http://chbookstore.qwestoffice.net/fa2006-08.html> (September 22, 2008).

6. Gregory Kirschling, "Stephenie Meyer: This Self-described 'Wuss' Has Legions of Devoted Readers Following Her Young-adult Novels," *Entertainment Weekly*, no. 947, August 10, 2007, p. 74.

7. Karen Valby, "Stephenie Meyer: 12 of My 'Twilight' Inspirations," *EW.com*, November 5, 2008, <http://www.ew.com/ew/gallery/0,,20237747,00.html?print> (November 9, 2008).

8. Lev Grossman, "Stephenie Meyer: A New J. K. Rowling?" *Time*, April 24, 2008, <http://www.time.com/time/magazine/article/0,9171,1734838-1,00.html> (January 15, 2008).

9. Irwin.

10. *Mormon.org*, s.v. "Agency," <http://mormon.org/mormonorg/eng/basic-beliefs/glossary/glossary-definition/agency> (December 28, 2008).

11. Stephenie Meyer, "Stephenie Meyer Q&A with TMs- Part 1 from 12/28/07," *Twilightmomsforum*, December 28, 2007, <http://twilightmomsforum.freeforums.org/stephenie-meyer-q-a-with-tms-part-1-from-12-28-07-t3222.html> (November 19, 2008).

12. Irwin.

13. Stephenie Meyer, "Unofficial Bio," *StephenieMeyer.com*, n.d., <http://www.stepheniemeyer.com/bio_unofficial.html> (September 22, 2008).

Chapter 5. Muse and Inspirations

1. Michael R. Walker, "A Teenage Tale With Bite," *BYU Magazine*, Winter 2007, <http://magazine.byu.edu/print.php?a=1972> (October 8, 2008).

2. Ibid.

3. Megan Irwin, "Charmed: Stephenie Meyer's Vampire Romance Novels Made a Mormon Mom an International Sensation," *Phoenix New Times*, July 12, 2007, <http://www.phoenixnewtimes.com/2007-07-12/news/charmed/> (November 19, 2008).

4. Ibid.

5. Cynthia Leitich Smith, "Author Interview: Stephenie Meyer on *Twilight*," March 27, 2006, <http://cynthialeitichsmith.blogspot.com/2006/03/author-interview-stephenie-meyer-on.html> (August 7, 2008).

6. Rick Margolis, "Love at First Bite." *School Library Journal*, vol. 51, no. 10, p. 37.

7. Irwin.

8. James Blasingame, "Interview With Stephenie Meyer," *Journal of Adolescent and Adult Literacy*, vol. 49, no. 7, April 2006, p. 631.

9. Smith.

10. *The Ellen DeGeneres Show* interview, Warner Bros. Studio, September 17, 2008.

11. "August Feature Article: Bookstories Interview With Stephenie Meyer," August 2006, <http://chbookstore.qwestoffice.net/fa2006-08.html> (September 22, 2008).

12. Linda M. Castellitto, "Dream of High School Vampires Inspire a Toothsome Debut," *BookPage*, October 2005, <http://www.bookpage.com/0510bp/stephenie_meyer.html> (August 7, 2008).

13. Ibid.

14. Blasingame, p. 631.

15. Ibid, p. 632.

16. Karen Valby, "Stephenie Meyer: 12 of My 'Twilight' Inspirations," *EW.com*, November 5, 2008, <http://www.ew.com/ew/gallery/0,,20237747,00.html?print> (November 9, 2008).

17. Ibid.

18. Ibid.

19. Blasingame, p. 631.

20. "History," *Quileute Nation*, n.d., <http://www.quileutenation.org/index.cfm?page=history.html> (November 12, 2008).

21. Blasingame, p. 632.

22. Stephenie Meyer, *Twilight* (New York: Little, Brown Books for Young Readers, 2005), p. 124.

23. Ibid., p. 125.

24. Valby.

25. Stephenie Meyer, "Unofficial Bio," *StephenieMeyer.com*, n.d., <http://www.stepheniemeyer.com/bio_unofficial.html> (September 22, 2008).

26. Valby.

Chapter 6. The Making of a Phenomenon

1. *The Ellen DeGeneres Show* interview, Warner Bros. Studio, September 17, 2008.
2. Stephenie Meyer, "Unofficial Bio," *StephenieMeyer.com*, n.d., <http://www.stepheniemeyer.com/bio_unofficial.html> (September 22, 2008).
3. *The Ellen DeGeneres Show* interview, Warner Bros. Studio, September 17, 2008.
4. Cynthia Leitich Smith, "Author Interview: Stephenie Meyer on Twilight," March 27, 2006, <http://cynthialeitichsmith.blogspot.com/2006/03/author-interview-stephenie-meyer-on.html> (August 7, 2008).
5. Ibid.
6. Megan Irwin, "Charmed: Stephenie Meyer's Vampire Romance Novels Made a Mormon Mom an International Sensation," *Phoenix New Times*, July 12, 2007, <http://www.phoenixnewtimes.com/2007-07-12/news/charmed/> (November 19, 2008).
7. Ibid.
8. Linda M. Castellitto, "Dream of High School Vampires Inspire a Toothsome Debut," October 2005, <http://www.bookpage.com/0510bp/stephenie_meyer.html> (August 7, 2008).
9. Ibid.
10. Karen Valby, "The Vampire Empire," *Entertainment Weekly*, July 18, 2008, p. 24.

11. "August Feature Article: Bookstories Interview With Stephenie Meyer," August 2006, <http://chbookstore.qwestoffice.net/fa2006-08.html> (September 22, 2008).

12. Ibid.

13. Stephenie Meyer, *Twilight* (New York: Little, Brown Books for Young Readers, 2005), p. 8.

14. Stephenie Meyer, e-mail correspondence with Sarah Moglia, November 2, 2005.

15. Stephenie Meyer, "Twilight FAQ," *StephenieMeyer.com*, n.d., <http://www.stepheniemeyer.com/*twilight*_faq.html> (September 22, 2008).

16. Hillias J. Martin et al., "Twilight," *School Library Journal*, vol. 51, no. 10, 2005, p. 166.

17. Sarah Moglia, author interview via e-mail, October 17, 2008.

18. Stephenie Meyer, e-mail correspondence with Sarah Moglia, November 2, 2005.

19. Valby, p. 27.

20. Irwin.

21. James Blasingame, "Interview With Stephenie Meyer," *Journal of Adolescent and Adult Literacy*, vol. 49, no. 7, April 2006, p. 631.

22. Brian Truitt, "The Twilight Zone," *USA Weekend*, November 14–16, 2008, p. 8.

23. Meyer, "Twilight FAQ."

24. Lev Grossman, "Stephenie Meyer: A New J. K. Rowling?" *Time*, April 24, 2008, <http://www.time.com/time/magazine/article/0,9171,1734838-1,00.html> (January 15, 2008).

25. Carol Memmott, "Meyer Unfazed as Fame Dawns," *USA Today*, July 31, 2008, p. 01D.

Chapter 7. Moon and Stars

1. "August Feature Article: Bookstories Interview With Stephenie Meyer," August 2006, <http://chbookstore.qwestoffice.net/fa2006-08.html> (September 22, 2008).

2. Karen Valby, "Stephenie Meyer: 12 of My 'Twilight' Inspirations," *EW.com*, November 5, 2008, <http://www.ew.com/ew/gallery/0,,20237747,00.html?print> (November 9, 2008).

3. Linda M. Castellitto, "Dreams of High School Vampires Inspire a Toothsome Debut," *BookPage*, October 2005, <http://www.bookpage.com/0510bp/stephenie_meyer.html> (September 22, 2008).

4. Stephenie Meyer, e-mail to Sarah Moglia, November 10, 2005.

5. Ibid.

6. Gregory Kirschling, "Stephenie Meyer: This Self-described 'Wuss' Has Legions of Devoted Readers Following Her Young-adult Novels," *Entertainment Weekly*, no. 947, August 10, 2007, p. 74.

7. James Blasingame, "Interview With Stephenie Meyer," *Journal of Adolescent and Adult Literacy*, vol. 49, no. 7, April 2006, p. 630.

8. Stephenie Meyer, *New Moon* (New York: Little, Brown and Company, Hachette Book Group USA, 2006), Acknowledgments.

9. Rick Margolis, "Love at First Bite." *School Library Journal*, vol. 51, no. 10, p. 37.

10. Megan Irwin, "Charmed: Stephenie Meyer's Vampire Romance Novels Made a Mormon Mom an International Sensation," *Phoenix New Times*, July 12, 2007, <http://www. phoenixnewtimes.com/2007-07-12/news/ charmed/> (November 19, 2008).

11. Sue Corbett, "Summer's Other Big-Deal Sequel," *People*, vol. 68, no. 8, August 20, 2007, p. 47.

12. "Eclipse," *Publishers Weekly*, vol. 254, no. 33, August 20, 2008, p. 69.

13. Gregory Kirschling, "Stephenie Meyer's 'Twilight' Zone," *EW.com*, August 2, 2008, <http://www.ew.com/ew/article/0,, 20049578,00.html> (September 22, 2008).

Chapter 8. Aliens, Vampires, and Fan Frenzy

1. Stephenie Meyer, "Author Interview," *Hachette Book Group*, n.d., <http://www. hachettebookgroup.com/9FA6868D6CC4417 38975A4C8D11EA37A.htm> (September 23, 2008).

2. Ibid.

3. Karen Valby, "The Vampire Empire," *Entertainment Weekly*, July 18, 2008, p. 26.

4. Jane Jorgenson, "The Host," *Library Journal*, vol. 133, no. 6, April 1, 2008, p. 77.

5. Carol Memmott, "'Twilight Author Sinks Her Teeth Into an Adult Tale," *USA Today*, May 6, 2008, p. 07d.

6. John Mark Eberhart, "Stephenie Meyer's Vampire Novels Were the Dawning of a Career," *Kansas City Star*, May 7, 2008, Newspaper Source, EBSCOhost (January 15, 2009).

7. "Meet Stephenie Meyer," *BookPage*, May 2008, <http://www.bookpage.com/0805bp/stephenie_meyer.html> (September 24, 2008).

8. Eli Sanders, "10 Questions for Stephenie Meyer," *Time*, August 21, 2008, <http://www.time.com/time/printout/0,8816,1834663,00.html> (September 9, 2008).

9. "Little, Brown Books for Young Readers Announces On-Sale Date of Highly-Anticipated Final Novel in Stephenie Meyer's Twilight Saga," *Reuters*, February 7, 2008, <http://www.reuters.com/article/pressRelease/idUS150361+07-Feb-2008+PRN20080207> (September 23, 2008).

10. Ibid.

11. John A. Sellers, "Big Week for (and Big Reactions to) 'Breaking Dawn,'" *Publishers Weekly*, August 7, 2008, <http://publishersweekly.com/index.asp?layout=articlePrint&articleID=CA6585318> (August 7, 2008).

12. "Breaking Dawn Concert Series Featuring Justin Furstenfeld of Blue October," *The Twilight Saga*, July 10, 2008, <http://www.the*twilight*saga.com/files/BD-ConcertSeries.pdf> (August 20, 2008).

13. Michael R. Walker, "A Teenage Tale With Bite," *BYU Magazine*, Winter 2007, <http://magazine.byu.edu/print.php?a=1972> (October 8, 2008).

14. Cara von Wrangel Kinsey, "Breaking Dawn," *School Library Journal*, vol. 54, no. 10, October 2008, p. 154.

15. Carol Memmott, "Meyer Unfazed as Fame Dawns," *USA Today*, July 31, 2008, p. 01D.

16. Karen Valby, "Stephenie Meyer Talks 'Twilight,'" *EW.com*, November 5, 2008, <http://www.ew.com/ew/article/0,, 20234559_20234567_20238527,00.html?print> (November 13, 2008).

Chapter 9. Lightning Strikes and Red Carpets

1. Linda M. Castellitto, "Dreams of High School Vampires Inspire a Toothsome Debut," *BookPage*, October 2005, <http://www.bookpage.com/0510bp/stephenie_meyer.html> (September 22, 2008).

2. Carol Memmott, "Meyer Unfazed as Fame Dawns," *USA Today*, July 31, 2008, p. 01D.

3. Michael R. Walker, "A Teenage Tale With Bite," *BYU Magazine*, Winter 2007, <http://magazine.byu.edu/print.php?a=1972> (October 8, 2008).

4. Stephenie Meyer, "Midnight Sun: Edward's Version of Twilight," *StephenieMeyer.com*, August 28, 2008, <http://www.stepheniemeyer.com/midnightsun.html> (September 2, 2008).

5. Ibid.

6. Ibid.

7. Ibid.

8. "August Feature Article: Bookstories Interview With Stephenie Meyer," August 2006, <http://chbookstore.qwestoffice.net/fa2006-08.html> (September 22, 2008).

9. Larry Carroll, "'Twilight' Tuesday: Catherine Hardwicke Gets Swept Up by Bella and Edward's 'Obsessive' Love," *MTV.com*, September 2, 2008, <http://www.mtv.com/movies/news/articles/1593892/story.jhtml> (September 14, 2008).

10. Lauren Waterman, "Vamped Up," *Teen Vogue*, December/January 2009, p. 172.

11. Ibid.

12. Nicole Sperling, "'Twilight' Hits Hollywood," *Entertainment Weekly*, July 18, 2008, p. 30.

13. Christina Radish, "Twilight's Author and Director Talk About Bringing the Film to Life," *MediaBlvd Magazine*, September 17, 2008, <http://www.mediablvd.com/magazine/the_news/celebrity/twilight%27s_author_and_director_talk_about_bringing_the_film_to_life_200809171287.html> (December 22, 2008).

14. Ibid.

15. Marc Malkin, "Twilight Scoop! Sequels, Action, and Paramore," *EOnline.com*, September 8, 2008, <http://www.eonline.com/uberblog/marc_malkin/b27859_twilight_scoop_sequels_action_paramore.html> (September 14, 2008).

16. Karen Valby, "Stephenie Meyer Talks 'Twilight,' *EW.com*, November 5, 2008, <http://www.ew.com/ew/article/0,,20234559_20234567_20238527,00.html?print> (November 13, 2008).

17. Brooks Barnes, "Box-Office Pulse: Blood Lust Runs Hot," *New York Times*, November 24, 2008, <http://www.nytime.com/2008/11/24/movies/24box.html?_r=1> (December 29, 2008).

18. Ibid.

19. Laura Saltman, "Dish of Salt: The Appeal of 'Twilights' Robert Pattinson," LA Premiere Interview Transcript, November 17, 2008, <http://www.accesshollywood.com/robert-pattinson-tops-ews-10-breakout-stars-of-2008_article_12259> (December 28, 2008).

20. Karen Valby, "The Vampire Empire," *Entertainment Weekly*, July 18, 2008, p. 27.

21. Valby, "Stephenie Meyer Talks 'Twilight.'"

22. Chris Cuomo, "Stephenie Meyer Interview," *Good Morning America* (ABC), July 31, 2008.

23. Stephenie Meyer, "Author Interview," *Hachette Book Group*, n.d., <http://www.hachettebookgroup.com/9FA6868D6CC441738975A4C8D11EA37A.htm> (September 23, 2008).

In Her Own Words

1. Gregory Kirschling, "Stephenie Meyer's "Twilight Zone," August 2, 2008, <http://www.ew.com/ew/article/0,,20049578,00.html> (September 22, 2008).

2. Michael R. Walker, "A Teenage Tale with Bite," *BYU Magazine*, Winter 2007, <http://magazine.byu.edu/print.php?a=1972.

3. Eli Sanders, "10 Questions," *Time*, vol. 172, Issue 9, September 1, 2008, p. 4.

4. Ibid.

5. "Author Interview—Stephenie Meyer," *StephenieMeyer.com*, n.d., <http://www.hachettebookgroup.com/9FA6868D6CC4417 38975A4C8D11EA37A.htm> (September 23, 2008).

6. Stephenie Meyer, "Twilight FAQ," *StephenieMeyer.com*, n.d., <http://www.stepheniemeyer.com/twilight_faq.html> (September 22, 2008).

7. Cynthia Leitich Smith, "Author Interview: Stephenie Meyer on Twilight," March 27, 2006, <http:cynthialeitichsmith.blogspot.com/2006/03/author-interview-stephenie-meyer-on-html> (August 7, 2008).

8. Christina Radish, "Twilight's Author and Director Talk About Bringing the Film to Life," September 17, 2008, <http://www.mediablvd.com/magazine/the_news/celebrity/twilight%27s_author_and_director_talk_about_bringing_the_film_to_life_200809171287.html> (December 22, 2008).

9. Chris Cuomo, "Stephenie Meyer Interview," *Good Morning America* (ABC), July 31, 2008.

Glossary

boutonniere—A flower or small bouquet worn on the lapel of a suit jacket.

civilized—Easy to manage or control; polite or well behaved.

compelled—Feeling a powerful and irresistible urge.

conservative—Traditional in style or manner.

counter offer—An offer made in response to an earlier offer made by another.

coven—A group or assembly.

debut—A first appearance.

descended—One's relationship to older generations or to an ancestor.

devised—Having formed a plan.

endeavor—An attempt or effort to succeed.

epilogue—A section at the end of a novel that concludes or completes the story.

eternal—Lasting forever; always existing.

hermit—Somebody who chooses to have little or no social contact.

heroine—A female lead character with heroic traits.

humanity—The state or condition of being human.

immortality—A state of unending life or existence.

manuscript—The original text of an author's work that is submitted to a publisher.

metaphor—A comparison using something to represent something else.

muse—A source of inspiration for artists, writers, and musicians.

nocturnal—Active at night.

query—A letter or inquiry to an editor written to gain interest in a manuscript.

rights—Interest or ownership.

surreal—Having a dreamlike quality; not feeling real.

query—A letter or inquiry to an editor written to gain interest of a manuscript.

sympathetic—Having caring and compassionate feelings.

truce—A temporary agreement to end disagreements.

voracious—Eager to consume large quantities.

Published Works of
Stephenie
Meyer

2005—*Twilight*

2006—*New Moon*

2007—*Prom Nights From Hell*

      Eclipse

2008—*The Host*

      Breaking Dawn

Further Reading

Vaz, Mark Cotta. *Twilight: The Complete Illustrated Movie Companion*. New York: Little, Brown and Company, 2008.

Gresh, Lois H. *The Twilight Companion: The Unauthorized Guide to the Series*. New York: St. Martin's Griffin, 2008.

Hopkins, Ellen. *A New Dawn: Your Favorite Authors on Stephenie Meyer's Twilight Series*. Dallas, Tex.: BenBella Books, 2008.

Internet Addresses

Stephenie Meyer's Web site
http://www.stepheniemeyer.com/

"Stephenie Meyer," Teenreads.com
http://www.teenreads.com/authors/
au-meyer-stephenie.asp

Twilight—The Official Movie Site
http://twilightthemovie.com/

Index